For My Gal Sal, one heck of a ballplayer —J.W.

For Carl and Leslie —B.B.

Text copyright © 2016 by Jonah Winter
Jacket art and interior illustrations copyright © 2016 by Barry Blitt
All rights reserved. Published in the United States by Schwartz & Wade Books, an imprint of Random House Children's Books, a division of Penguin Random House LLC, New York.

Schwartz & Wade Books and the colophon are trademarks of Penguin Random House LLC.

Visit us on the Web! randomhousekids.com

Educators and librarians, for a variety of teaching tools, visit us at RHTeachersLibrarians.com

Library of Congress Cataloging-in-Publication Data
Winter, Jonah.
You never heard of Casey Stengel?! / Jonah Winter, Barry Blitt.
pages cm.
ISBN 978-0-375-87013-2 (trade) — ISBN 978-0-375-97013-9 (glb) — ISBN 978-0-375-98748-9 (ebook)
1. Stengel, Casey—Juvenile literature. 2. Baseball managers—United States—Biography—Juvenile literature.
3. New York Yankees (Baseball team)—Juvenile literature. I. Blitt, Barry, ill. II. Title.
GV865.S8 W56 2015
796.357092—dc23
[B]
2014005746

The text of this book is set in Altma Serif.
The illustrations are rendered in pen-and-ink and watercolor.
Book design by Rachael Cole and Brianne Farley

MANUFACTURED IN CHINA

10 9 8 7 6 5 4 3 2 1

First Edition

YOU NEVER HEARD OF
CASEY STENGEL?!

WRITTEN BY JONAH WINTER   **ILLUSTRATED BY BARRY BLITT**

schwartz & wade books · new york

You never heard of *Casey Stengel*?! But you *must've* heard of "Casey at the Bat," right? About the mighty baseball player who breaks the hearts of all his fans by striking out? Well, this story's about another Casey. This Casey wasn't all that mighty, and no one expected him to do much of anything *but* strike out. Boy, did he show *them,* though—*even if it took him half a century to do it!*

Casey grew up with the name Charles Dillon Stengel in Kansas City, Missouri, smack-dab in America's heartland, back in the late 1800s, when people still rode in horse-drawn buggies.

And like most American boys back in those days, he only ever wanted to be one thing—*a baseball player.*

Okay, well, there was that one time when he wanted to be a dentist. But he decided against it, on account of the fact he was a lefty, he said, and all the dental tools were for right-handers. And so this left-handed, bowlegged, wisecracking character started playing baseball, traveling from one bush-league town to the next with his cardboard suitcase and big dreams of someday making the majors . . .

which he did, in 1912, signed by the . . . *seventh-place Brooklyn Dodgers.* Whaddayagonnado? His teammates did give him his nickname, though: K.C. (short for his hometown), which got turned into Casey. But after five years, they booted him.

Oh, but he did have his moments, especially as a New York Giant. Like the time he outhit Babe Ruth in the 1923 World Series, slamming two game-winning homers, including one inside-the-park home run that he somehow managed to score on, despite the fact that his left shoe kept almost falling off, causing him to hobble around the bases like an old, bowlegged sailor.

Here was the problem: Casey's skills at playing *baseball* were always overshadowed by his even greater skills at being a *goofball*. The stories of his goofballery are legendary: like the time he tipped his cap to some fans who were booing him, and out flew a sparrow.

Or the time he climbed into a manhole in the outfield . . . and leapt out to catch a fly ball.

Or the time when he got blamed for giving a pilot some grapefruits to drop on his manager. Casey was not taken seriously. And after fourteen years in the majors, he found himself out of a job—and without much to show for it but some funny stories.

What do you do when the one thing you love in life is taken away? Go to dental school? But what if you're a lefty?! If you're Casey, you become a manager—of a minor league team called the Toledo Mud Hens. It sounds kind of sad, and it was. For starters, the Mud Hens stank.

And managing baseball is hard on the brain. A manager has to take a roster of twenty-four to forty guys—and then decide which nine guys to put on the field. He decides the batting order. He says who pitches, and when that pitcher needs to be yanked. He tells his players when to bunt and when to steal. He tells his fielders where to stand for every single batter. If you think about it, a manager is the most important guy on the team—his decisions can make the difference between a win and a loss:

Bottom of the eighth. Your team's at bat. Two outs. Down by one run. You've got a guy on first. If he can score, the game is tied. So do you give the go-ahead sign for the steal? Suddenly, it was Casey's job to make that call. In every game he ever played, he'd been paying attention, taking mental notes. Now he had a chance to really *prove* what he'd learned.

Well. One of the first things he did as Mud Hens' manager was to walk onto the field without his pants. After fans started hooting and hollering, Casey finally looked down and said, "Why, I haven't got my pants on."

He wasn't trying to be funny. He just forgot!

	YEARS	TEAM	STANDING
CASEY'S MAJOR LEAGUE **MANAGERIAL RECORD** BEFORE 1949	1934	Brooklyn Dodgers	6th Place
	1935	Brooklyn Dodgers	5th Place
	1936	Brooklyn Dodgers	7th Place
	1938	Boston Bees	5th Place
	1939–42	Boston Bees/Braves (same team—used different names)	7th Place
	1943	Boston Braves	6th Place

It's nearly impossible to manage a bad team to victory. And as luck would have it, most of the teams Casey managed were terrible. For sixteen long years, he mainly looked out from the dugout at one bad team after the next: the Brooklyn Dodgers, the Boston Braves, the minor league Kansas City Blues. . . . It was hard. It was exhausting. As much as he hated to admit it, Casey started feeling old—like a failure, a chump.

THE NEW YORK YANKEES

The New York Yankees are the greatest team in the history of sports—and, for this reason, the most hated (by fans of other teams). They hold the major league records for most World Series wins (27) and most pennants (40). Many of their great players from long ago are still household names: Babe Ruth, Lou Gehrig, Joe DiMaggio, Mickey Mantle. The Yankees' owners have mainly cared about one thing: winning. The fact that they hired Casey Stengel is still seen as the wildest curveball in Yankees history.

Sometimes, though, just when you're about to give up, something amazing happens:

Call it a lucky break. Well, Casey scores TWO of these. First, he *finally* gets asked to manage a couple of *good* teams in the minors—first the Milwaukee Brewers, then the practically major league Oakland Oaks, which he leads to pennants in '44 and '48. But *now* . . . comes the *miracle.*

Casey gets a call from an old pal who works for the New York Yankees. He sees something in Casey that not too many others in the baseball universe see. He sees some special *quality* that he can't quite pin down, some potential for *greatness.* And, well, let's just cut to the chase.

On October 12, 1948, the Yanks—the greatest team in baseball history—hold a press conference. That year, they'd finished in third place—unacceptable by Yankee standards. And so they decide to shake things up by hiring a new manager: *Casey . . .* [gulp] *Stengel . . . ?*

Reporters drop their pens. Furniture falls from the sky. Clocks stop running. Dogs start speaking Italian and wearing fancy clothes. And then things really get weird.

YANKS HIRE CLOWN reads one headline. And all over the papers there's this picture of Casey staring into a baseball . . . as if it were a crystal ball and he a fortune-teller.

Who knows what Casey was "predicting," but Yankees fans were predicting the End of the World. Stengel was just a lovable goofball from the Olden Days of Baseball—how on earth was this daffy codger supposed to manage *THE* New York Yankees?

And most of the team thought he was a crazy fool—partly because Casey had a funny way of saying things that didn't always make sense. "All right," he once said, "everybody line up alphabetically according to your height." Some guys chuckled. Others scratched their heads.

Joe DiMaggio, the Yanks' superstar, wouldn't even look in Casey's direction. This was a bad situation. Still, there's only one thing you can do when nobody believes in you:

JOE DIMAGGIO

When Casey Stengel joined the Yankees, Joe DiMaggio was still arguably the biggest star in baseball. The "Yankee Clipper," as he was known, has often been called one of the greatest all-around players in history—his hitting, slugging, baserunning, throwing, and fielding were legendary. All over America, kids imitated his "wide stance" at the plate. People spoke of his grace, dignity, class. He was the opposite of Casey Stengel in pretty much every way. As fate would have it, he was at the end of his career when Casey took over.

Act like an even crazier fool! Woo-hoo! Actually, Casey wasn't *trying* to be a crazy fool; it just seemed that way. He wasn't afraid to take a chance with new things—like moving guys in and out of the lineup, game to game, inning to inning, for no apparent reason.

Except, there *was* a reason. Casey Stengel wanted every single player to play. Why just use the same nine guys every day? That was how most managers managed—and it was dumb. What if those guys get hurt? Then you've got to stick in some replacement from the bench who's out of practice. Dumb.

Casey trained each guy to play a few positions. No matter who got injured, you always had a backup. And let's say your first baseman is a lefty, but what you need now is a righty to face the lefty pitcher. Well, if you've got other guys who can play first base, you just pull some righty first baseman off the bench and—presto!—problem solved. Whoever's pitching, righty or lefty, you use the opposite to face him. This is called "platooning"—an old-timey baseball strategy that Casey was old and wise enough to bring back. SMART!

This strategy had the added advantage of confusing other teams. Other managers never knew which nine Yankees they'd be facing during any given inning. Casey's not-so-crazy logic kept his Bronx Bombers on top for most of 1949—

That is, until the last week of the season, when they slipped into second place. Of course, no one was surprised. Everyone had expected Casey to fail. He was simply not up to the job of managing a first-rate team, they said.

YANKEES/RED SOX RIVALRY

The Yankees/Red Sox rivalry is one of the oldest and most intense in baseball history. Before 1920, the Red Sox won five World Series. Then they sold their star pitcher, Babe Ruth, to the Yankees. Oopsie. The Yankees promptly discovered that "The Bambino" was an even better hitter than he was a pitcher. With Babe Ruth, they turned into the dominant team—and stayed dominant long after his departure. The Red Sox, though often great, would not win another World Series until 2004. Baseball historians call this "The Curse of the Bambino." And Red Sox fans . . . well, let's put it this way: they don't much like the Yankees.

CRRRR

Of course, "they" have been known to be wrong.

October 2, 1949, the last game of the year, the Yankees are still alive, battling their archrivals, the Boston Red Sox, for the pennant. It's looking good. The Yanks have their ace, Vic Raschi, on the mound. Raschi's a big guy who snarls at batters and wins games. And today, he's kept Beantown scoreless through eight innings. Yanks are up five–zip. Top of the ninth.

All the Yankees need are three more outs and they win the pennant. But suddenly Raschi gives up a walk, a single, and a triple. Two runs score. Then Raschi gives up another hit—and another run. Just like that, the Red Sox put three runs on the board. Score is now five–three. Two outs.

What do you do if you're Casey Stengel? Raschi's been pitching for eight and two-thirds innings—maybe he's tired. Maybe it's time for a reliever. On the other hand, he's a "big game" pitcher who does best when the stakes are high. If you make a mistake and the Yankees lose, you will be forever blamed. Everything is on the line—the pennant, your job, your place in history. And you've got five seconds to make up your mind.

Good managers make good decisions—split-second decisions—sometimes because of nothing more than a gut feeling. But those feelings are based on a lifetime of watching and thinking and living and breathing baseball. Casey's brain was like a computer containing thousands upon thousands of baseball moments—which helped him predict the outcome of each choice. And though maybe he couldn't say exactly why, *he keeps Raschi in the game.*

The Red Sox's next batter, Birdie Tebbetts, steps up to the plate. In comes the ball. Tebbetts CONNECTS

but pops it up in foul territory. First baseman Tommy Henrich races over to catch it

. . . for the final out! Yankees win the pennant! With none other than *Casey Stengel* at the helm! Take THAT, New York! Take THAT, you doubters! Who's laughing NOW?!

And this is just the beginning. If success is the best revenge, Casey sure does get even. For twelve golden years, Casey leads the Yankees to *TEN* pennants and *SEVEN World Series wins*. And that includes *FIVE World Series wins in a row—* a record that still stands.

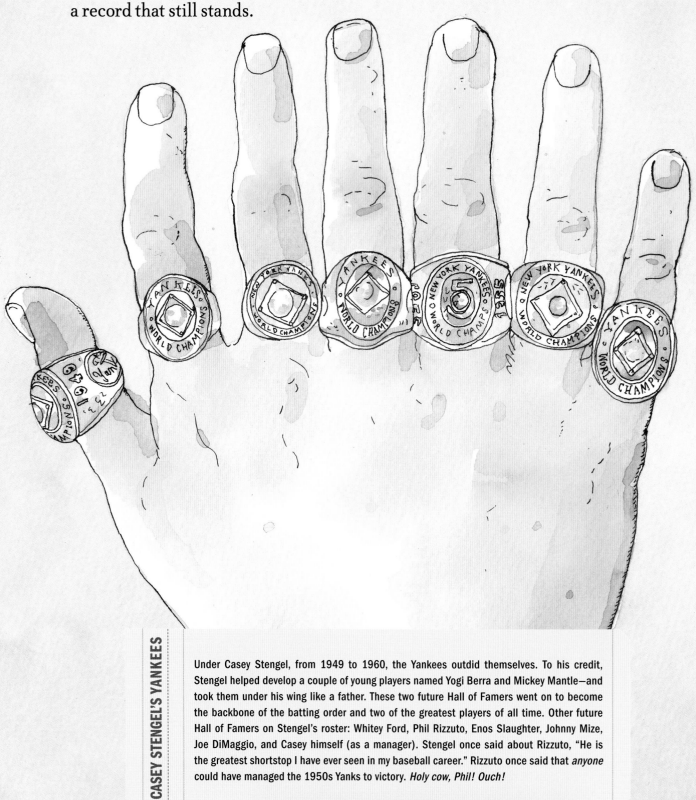

CASEY STENGEL'S YANKEES

Under Casey Stengel, from 1949 to 1960, the Yankees outdid themselves. To his credit, Stengel helped develop a couple of young players named Yogi Berra and Mickey Mantle—and took them under his wing like a father. These two future Hall of Famers went on to become the backbone of the batting order and two of the greatest players of all time. Other future Hall of Famers on Stengel's roster: Whitey Ford, Phil Rizzuto, Enos Slaughter, Johnny Mize, Joe DiMaggio, and Casey himself (as a manager). Stengel once said about Rizzuto, "He is the greatest shortstop I have ever seen in my baseball career." Rizzuto once said that *anyone* could have managed the 1950s Yanks to victory. *Holy cow, Phil! Ouch!*

But baseball is more than just numbers and stats. What Casey Stengel was cannot be summed up in wins or losses. For twelve amazing years, Casey was the center of the Yankees. And the Yankees were the center of New York. And New York, with its three great teams—the Yankees, the Giants, and the Dodgers—was the center of baseball. And during the 1950s, baseball was the center of the universe. This could only mean: *Casey Stengel was the Center of the Universe.*

"Good pitching will always stop good hitting, and vice versa."

"The team has come along slow but fast."

"I was not successful as a ballplayer, as it was a game of skill."

"If we're going to win the pennant, we've got to start thinking we're not as good as we think we are."

"The secret of managing is to keep the guys who hate you away from the guys who are undecided."

Or at least, he was pretty good at acting the part. Now he had the biggest stage you could imagine, performing for anyone who'd listen, talking and talking and talking—which is how he earned his nickname, the Old Perfessor. Without even cracking a smile, he made people laugh: "There comes a time in every man's life, and I've had plenty of 'em," he once famously said. What did it mean? No one was sure, and so they called it Stengelese.

Late into the night, Casey rambled on about baseball. It was all he thought about, all he cared about. And if you could get past his Stengelese—and stay awake—you'd realize that he wasn't speaking nonsense. He had memorized every single scouting report for every single player in the league. After half a century in baseball, he was a walking, talking *encyclopedia* of the game.

CASEY STENGEL'S MANAGERIAL RECORD 1949–1960

WINS	LOSSES	W-L%	WORLD SERIES WINS	PENNANTS
1,149	696	.623	7	10

So you see, Casey Stengel was much more than just a clown. But he was also much more than a great manager. Casey Stengel, in his own goofy way, was a wise man. He knew how to win *and* how to lose—without taking himself too seriously. *For heaven's sake, the guy even knew how to get booed!* You know how to get booed? You turn straight toward the crowd with a great big smile, like he did after winning his last World Series in Milwaukee. And as those fans start booing even louder . . . you blow 'em a great big kiss.

And somewhere, someone's radio is playing . . .
"Ha ha ha! Who's got the last laugh now!"

GLOSSARY OF BASEBALL TERMS

American League: One of the two groups of teams in Major League Baseball.

Batting average: Number of hits divided by times at bat.

Batting stance: The way a batter stands at the plate.

Beantown: Nickname for Boston, famous for its "Boston-baked beans."

Bench: The place where players not currently in the lineup are sitting.

"Casey at the Bat": A famous poem from the 1800s about a fictional baseball star named Casey who strikes out and in so doing causes much sadness in the town of Mudville.

Dodgers: One of the oldest teams in baseball, founded in 1884, originally called the Atlantics (then the Grays, the Bridegrooms, the Grooms, the Superbas, the Trolley Dodgers, and the Robins), which played in Brooklyn until 1957 and then moved to Los Angeles.

Giants: One of the oldest National League teams, founded in 1883 and originally called the Gothams (until 1885). They played in New York until 1957 and then moved to San Francisco.

Hall of Famer: A baseball player or manager so great as to have been inducted into the National Baseball Hall of Fame (after his career is over).

Hit: When a batter connects with the ball and makes it safely to one of the bases.

Home run: A hit in which the batter circles all four bases and scores a run.

Inside-the-park home run: A home run in which the ball touches the ground in fair territory.

Lineup: The nine players officially representing the team at any given point during a game.

National League: The older of the two groups of teams in Major League Baseball.

Pennant: The championship title for each league, determining which two teams go on to the World Series.

Platooning: A managerial strategy by which at least one lefty and one righty plays a given position—and can be pulled in or out of the lineup for the purpose of pitting a lefty hitter against a righty pitcher and vice versa.

RBIs (runs batted in): Runs that are the result of a player's at-bat (even if the ball is caught or the player is tagged out), except in instances resulting from an error or a double play.

Red Sox: One of the original American League teams, founded in 1901, originally called the Americans (until 1908), which has always played in Boston.

Reliever: A pitcher who enters the game after the starting pitcher has been removed.

Roster: The official list of all the players who comprise a team at any given point.

Routine pop fly: A fly ball that should be caught by a fielder.

Scouting report: A report outlining a player's strengths and weaknesses—sometimes against specific pitchers or hitters.

Steal: When a base runner moves safely to the next base while the pitcher is pitching or about to pitch the ball.

World Series: The best-of-seven championship series played by the National League and the American League pennant winners.

ABOUT THE STATISTICS IN THIS BOOK

Here are the online resources from which my statistics come:

baseball-almanac.com

baseballhalloffame.org

baseballlibrary.com

baseball-references.com

Baseball statistics have always been and will always be interpreted differently by different fans and scholars. Often, several fans will use the same set of statistics to come up with entirely different top-ten lists. This is a very subjective and sentimental process, not an exact science. And the arguments that inevitably arise are as much a part of the baseball tradition as peanuts and Cracker Jack.

AUTHOR'S NOTE

Casey Stengel's life was far too long and interesting to tell it all in a picture book. Though this book ends with his wonderful years with the Yankees, Casey's career did not end here. After the 1960 season, when Casey had just turned seventy years old, the Yankees fired him. Casey quipped, "I'll never make the mistake of being seventy again." Two years later, he was hired to manage a brand-new team called the New York Mets—and during his four years with the Mets, they were the worst team in baseball history. Nonetheless, Stengel was beloved in New York for his charming personality and his success with the Yankees, and people came to see the Mets just to see the "Old Perfessor" make them laugh with his never-ending antics. About the Mets, he said, "Been in this game one hundred years, but I see new ways to lose 'em I never knew existed before." He finally left the game of baseball for good in 1965, at the age of seventy-five. He died of cancer ten years later on September 29, 1975, in Glendale, California. And he is still missed. They just don't make 'em like Casey Stengel anymore.

CASEY
STENGEL